eisure &
EE

to Knit

Sachiyo Ishii

Search Press

First published in 2016

Search Press Limited
Wellwood, North Farm Road,
Tunbridge Wells, Kent TN2 3DR

Text copyright © Sachiyo Ishii 2016

Photographs by Paul Bricknell at
Search Press Studios

Photographs and design copyright
© Search Press Ltd 2016

Print ISBN: 978-1-78221-252-2
ebook ISBN: 978-1-78126-298-6

The Publishers and author can accept no
responsibility for any consequences arising from
the information, advice or instructions given in
this publication.

Readers are permitted to reproduce any of the
items in this book for their personal use, or for
the purposes of selling for charity, free of charge
and without the prior permission of the Publishers.
Any use of the items for commercial purposes is
not permitted without the prior permission of
the Publishers.

Suppliers
If you have difficulty in obtaining any of the
materials and equipment mentioned in this book,
then please visit the Search Press website for
details of suppliers: www.searchpress.com

Printed in China

Dedication
*I would like to dedicate this book to
my sister, who has supported me and
given me lots of encouragement.*

Abbreviations

beg:	beginning
dec:	decrease
DPN:	double-pointed needles
g st:	garter stitch: knit every row
inc:	increase (by working into the front and back of the same stitch)
k:	knit
k2tog:	knit 2 stitches together
knitwise:	as though to knit
m1:	make 1 stitch by picking up the horizontal yarn before the next st and knitting into the back of it
p:	purl
p2tog:	purl 2 stitches together
p3tog:	purl 3 stitches together
psso:	pass slipped stitch over
purlwise:	as though to purl
rem:	remaining
rep:	repeat
RS:	right side/s
sl:	slip, usually slip 1 stitch
skpo:	slip 1 stitch, knit 1 stitch, pass slipped stitch over
st(s):	stitch(es)
st st:	stocking stitch (US stockinette stitch); alternate knit and purl rows (unless directed otherwise, always start with a knit row)
WS:	wrong side/s
ybk:	yarn back (between needles)
yfwd:	yarn forward (between needles)

Contents

Introduction

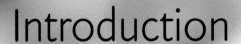

One of the obstacles for a beginner knitter is often making large items with lots of stitches and rows, which have to be neat and even. Some people find it daunting, some find it too time-consuming and others find it boring. I know exactly how it feels, because I have been there myself. I almost decided that knitting was not for me and wanted to give up altogether.

But with these tiny toys, you can enjoy the delight of accomplishment in just a few hours! I have found that this motivates me to create, and I hope it will do the same for you. The knitting skills you need to make these tiny toys are quite basic and you don't have to worry too much about making mistakes – the projects are very forgiving. Most of them require very little yarn and are perfect for using up scraps in your stash, so you don't need to invest much at all.

These toys are perfect for small hands and easily carried in your bag – childen will love to play with them. You could also attach a string and tie one to your bag as a charm dangle, or you can display them as ornaments. There are many ways to enjoy them and there is something for everyone.

I am sure you can make many people smile with these little creations. Knitting isn't only about making sweaters and I hope you enjoy making these projects as much as I did.

Happy knitting!

Knitting know-how

Yarn

All the toys in this book are knitted with double knitting (DK/8-ply) yarn. You do not need much yarn to create each toy. Some require less than 10m (11yd) of yarn, which is approximately equivalent to a skein of tapestry wool. These toys are perfect for using up yarn already in your stash. I prefer to knit with DK (8-ply) yarn, but you can use any weight of yarn you like – just remember to adjust the needle size accordingly.

I have used mainly 100 per cent wool yarns in the projects, as I love the feel of wool and the subtle colour tones it can create. If you are making toys for children, you might wish to choose natural materials. I also find wool is the easiest when you want to make stitches neat and even. Feel free to experiment with alpaca, mohair, cotton or synthetic yarns for different textures. I have also used chunky, fleecy yarn for some projects. This can be replaced with mohair or boucle yarn if you prefer. If you need only small quantities of certain colours, tapestry yarn is a good choice.

Stuffing

I usually use washed wool fleece to stuff toys. It is not finely carded Merino-type wool for wet felting and is inexpensive. I have found it ideal

1 Tapestry wool
2 DK (8-ply) yarn
3 Chunky-weight, fleecy yarn
4 Carded washed wool fleece
5 Uncarded washed wool fleece
6 Toy stuffing
7 Knitting needles
8 Chopstick
9 Tapestry needles
10 Scissors

for stuffing toys as it is natural, has plenty of bounce, and fills any shape well. If you cannot get hold of wool fleece, you can use polyester toy filling, which is readily available from most craft shops and online craft stores.

Knitting needles

All the toys in this book were made using double-pointed 2.75mm (US 2, UK 12) knitting needles. Your knitting tension needs to be fairly tight so that when the toys are sewn up, the toy stuffing is not visible through the stitches. If you find that you struggle to knit with DK (8-ply) yarn on fine needles, experiment with slightly larger needles. Some knitters knit more tightly than others, and the tension can also differ depending on the yarn you use. I have not specified tension for any of the projects, as the size of the finished toys does not really matter.

Crochet hook

You will also need a size 3mm (US C/2 or D/3, UK 11) crochet hook. This is used to make chains and pick up stitches from a knitted piece. You do not need to know how to crochet to make the projects in this book.

Sewing your work together

I recommend that you use a chenille or tapestry needle with a sharp point, as it is easier to work through your tightly knitted toys than a blunt-ended needle. You can also use the same needle for embroidering features on the toys. Your toys will be sewn up using the same yarn that you knitted them with, so it is a good idea to make a habit of leaving fairly long yarn ends when you cast on and cast off. Join the seams using mattress stitch with right sides facing outwards.

Other tools

Wooden chopstick

A simple but incredibly effective tool, a chopstick is by far the best instrument for pushing stuffing into your toys. If you do not have one, you could use a large knitting needle or a pencil.

Scissors

Essential for trimming yarn ends when sewing up your projects.

Stitches used

Unless specified otherwise, all patterns are worked in stocking stitch. Other stitches used for making features for the toys are described below and are extremely simple. They include i-cords, French knots and backstitch.

I-cords

I-cords are used for some of the animal body parts including the cat's tail (see page 8) and the piggy's legs (see page 24). Using double-pointed needles, cast on the required number of stitches. Do not turn. Slide the stitches to the opposite end of the needle, then knit the stitches again, taking the yarn firmly across the back of the work. Repeat to the desired length. Cast off.

French knots

These are used for most of the animals' eyes. Take the needle through the yarn, separating the fibres instead of taking the needle out between the stitches. This prevents the eye from sinking into the face.

Backstitch

This stitch is used to make small body parts, such as the sheep's nose (see page 16). Thread the yarn through the needle. Bring the needle to the front of the work. Insert the needle from front to back and repeat. If you work on the same spot, you can build up small body parts with yarn, such as the guardsman's nose on page 22 and the clown's nose on page 46. You can also create hair with backstitch by leaving long loops, such as the boy angel's hair in the photograph below (see also page 42).

Materials:

Small amounts of DK (8-ply) yarn in black, white and brown

Small amount of 4-ply (fingering) yarn in white

Small amount of toy stuffing

Approximate size:

5cm (2in) high

Instructions:

Body

Starting with the base, cast on 6 sts using black yarn.

Row 1 (WS): p.

Row 2: inc to end (12 sts).

Row 3: p.

Row 4: (k1, inc) to end (18 sts).

Rows 5–11: st st, starting with a p row.

Row 12 (shape neck): (k1, k2tog) to end (12 sts).

Row 13: p.

Row 14: k1, (inc) to last st, k1 (22 sts).

Rows 15–21: st st, starting with a p row.

Cast off.

Tail

Cast on 3 sts and work an i-cord for 10 rows. Break yarn, draw through sts, pull tightly and fasten off.

Eyes (make two)

Using 4-ply (fingering) white yarn, (or two strands taken from white DK (8-ply) yarn), cast on 8 sts, break yarn, draw through sts, pull tightly and fasten off.

Making up

Using the cast-on end of the yarn, work a gathering thread along this edge and draw in tightly. Sew the rest of the body seam, leaving the top open. Stuff the body, avoiding the neck area. With the body seam at the back, sew the top of the head together at right angles to the back seam. Sew the corner of the head, across the front and back pieces to create triangular ears. Work a gathering thread around the neck, then pull tightly to shape the neck. To flatten the base, insert a threaded needle into the base centre and take it out through the back of the neck and repeat. Pull gently. Attach the white eyes, then add French knots to the centre of the eyes using dark brown or black yarn. Embroider the nose in brown using small backstitches.

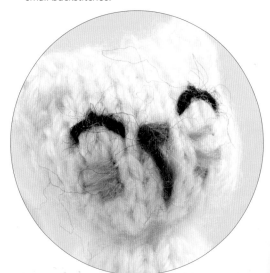

To make the white cat, work the head and body in white yarn as for the black cat, then embroider the eyes in dark brown, the nose and mouth in brown and the whiskers in coral, using the photograph opposite for guidance.

Teddy Bear

Materials:

Small amounts of DK (8-ply) yarn in white, dark brown, pale pink and pink

Small amount of toy stuffing

Approximate size:

6cm (2⅜ in) high

Instructions:

Body

The body is knitted in st st with a colour pattern. Do not break yarn each time to change colours. Use the yarn ends left from the previous rows.

Starting with the base, cast on 8 sts using pink yarn.

Row 1 (WS): p.

Row 2: inc in each st (16 sts).

Row 3: p.

Row 4: (k1, inc) to end (24 sts).

Row 5: using pale pink, p.

Row 6: using pale pink, k.

Row 7: using pink, p.

Rows 8 and 9: move sts to other end of DPN, rep rows 5 and 6.

Row 10: move sts to other end of DPN, using pink yarn, k.

Rows 11–16: repeat rows 5–10, working two rows in pale pink yarn, one row in pink, finishing the last row in pink.

Rows 17–26: change to white yarn and work in st st, starting with a p row.

Row 27: (k2, k2tog) to end (18 sts).

Row 28: (p1, p2tog) to end (12 sts).

Break yarn, draw through sts, pull tightly and fasten off.

Ears (make two)

Cast on 10 sts using white yarn. Break yarn, draw through sts, pull tightly and fasten off.

Muzzle

Cast on 12 sts using white yarn and p 1 row. Break yarn, draw through sts, pull tightly and fasten off.

Arms and legs (make four)

Cast on 6 sts using white yarn and work in st st for 5 rows. Break yarn, draw through sts, then pull tightly and fasten off.

Making up

Sew the body seam and stuff. Attach the muzzle with a little stuffing if needed. Attach the ears. Sew the seam of the arms and legs, starting with the cast-off ends, and close the seam without stuffing. Attach them to the body. Using dark brown yarn, work French knots for the eyes. Using two strands taken from the dark brown yarn, create a nose with two short backstitches and the mouth with one long, vertical backstitch.

To make the blue teddy bear, work the pattern as for the pink bear, using blue where pink yarn is specified and light blue where pale pink yarn is specified.

Rocket

Materials:

Approx. 10m (11yd) of DK (8-ply) yarn in light purple or blue

Small amounts of DK (8-ply) yarn in cream, white and light grey

Small amount of toy stuffing

Additional equipment:

3mm (US C/2 or D/3, UK 11) crochet hook

Approximate size:

8cm (3⅛in) high

Instructions:

Body

Starting with the tail, cast on 6 sts using light purple yarn.

Row 1 (WS): p.

Row 2: inc in each st (12 sts).

Row 3: p.

Row 4: (k1, inc) to end (18 sts).

Row 5: p.

Row 6: (k2, inc) to end (24 sts).

Rows 7–16: st st, starting with a p row.

Rows 17 and 18: change to cream yarn and st st, starting with a p row.

Row 19: (p2, p2tog) to end (18 sts).

Rows 20–22: st st.

Row 23: (p2, p2tog) to last 2 sts, p2 (14 sts).

Rows 24–26: st st.

Row 27: (p2tog) to end (7 sts).

Break yarn, draw through sts, pull tight and fasten off.

Tail wings (make four)

Cast on 4 sts with light purple yarn.

Rows 1–4: st st.

Row 5: k to last st, inc (5 sts).

Row 6: p.

Row 7: k.

Row 8: k for fold line.

Row 9: k.

Row 10: p.

Row 11: k to last 2 sts, k2tog (4 sts).

Rows 12–15: st st, starting with a p row.

Cast off.

Window

Cast on 10 sts using light grey yarn and p 1 row. Break yarn, draw through sts, pull tight and fasten off.

Top point

Cast on 2 sts using light purple yarn and work an i-cord for 2 rows. Fasten off.

Making up

Sew the body seam, stuff and close the seam, with the top point inside the seam. Fold the tail wings at the folding line, then sew the sides and attach them to the body. Attach the window. Using white yarn, work 15 chains with the crochet hook and attach this around the window. Make another chain of 30 using white yarn and attach around the body where the colour changes.

Lucky Owls

Materials:

Small amounts of DK (8-ply) yarn in white, yellow, dark brown, coral and green

Small amount of toy stuffing

Approximate size:

Large: 5cm (2in) high; small: 4.5cm (1¾in) high

Instructions:

Large owl's body

Starting with the base, cast on 8 sts using green yarn.

Row 1 (WS): p.

Row 2: inc in each st (16 sts).

Row 3: p.

Row 4: (k1, inc) to end (24 sts).

Row 5: p8 (green), p8 (white), p8 (green).

Rows 6 and 7: keeping the colours as set, st st.

Row 8: k8 (green), [(k1 (white), k1 (green)] four times, k8 (green).

Row 9: p8 (green), [p1 (white), p1 (green)] four times, p8 (green).

Rows 10 and 11: as row 8–9. Fasten off white yarn.

Row 12: (k2, k2tog) to end (18 sts).

Rows 13–18: st st, starting with a p row.

Row 19: p6, (p2tog) three times, p to end (15 sts).

Cast off.

Wings (make two)

Cast on 10 sts using green yarn.

Rows 1–3: st st, starting with a p row.

Row 4: k2, (k2tog, k2) to end (8 sts).

Rows 5 and 6: st st, starting with a p row.

Break yarn, draw through sts, pull tightly and fasten off.

Eyes (make two)

Using white yarn, cast on 10 sts, break yarn. Draw through sts, pull tightly and fasten off.

Feet (make two)

Cast on 4 sts using yellow.

Rows 1 and 2: k.

Row 3: k1, k2tog, k1 (3 sts).

Row 4: p.

Break yarn, draw through sts, pull tightly and fasten off.

Beak

Cast on 5 sts using yellow yarn.

Row 1 (WS): p2tog, p1, p2tog (3 sts).

Row 2: sl1, k2tog, psso and fasten off.

Making up

Work a gathering thread through each stitch of the body's cast-on edge and draw up tightly. Sew up the body seam to half way. Keeping the seam in the centre of the back, sew the top of the head with overcast stitching. Stuff the body and close the seam. Seam each wing and attach to the body without stuffing. Attach the eyes, beak and feet to the body. Add centres to the eyes with a French knot using dark brown yarn.

Small owl's body

Cast on 7 sts using coral yarn.

Row 1 (WS): p.

Row 2: inc in each st (14 sts).

Row 3: p.

Row 4: (k1, inc) to end (21 sts).

Row 5: p7 (coral), p7 (white), p7 (coral).

Rows 6 and 7: keeping the colours as set, st st.

Row 8: k7 (coral), [k1 (white), k1 (coral)] three times, k1 (white), k7 (coral).

Row 9: p7 (coral), [p1 (pink), p1 (white)] three times, p8 (coral).

Rows 10 and 11: as rows 8 and 9. Break white yarn.

Row 12: (k2, k2tog) to last st, k1 (16 sts).

Rows 13–17: st st, starting with a p row.

Row 18: k5, (k2tog) three times, k5 (13 sts).

Cast off.

Wings (make two)

Cast on 9 sts using coral yarn.

Rows 1and 2: st st, starting with a p row.

Row 3: (p2, p2tog) twice, p1 (7 sts).

Rows 4 and 5: st st.

Break yarn, draw through sts, pull tightly and fasten off.

Eyes (make two)

Cast on 9 sts using white yarn, break yarn, draw through sts, pull tightly and fasten off.

Feet (make two)

Cast on 3 sts using yellow yarn.

Row 1: k.

Row 2: sl1, k2tog (2 sts).

Row 3: p.

Break yarn, draw through sts, pull tightly and fasten off.

Beak

Cast on 4 sts using yellow yarn.

Row 1 (WS): p1, p2tog, p1 (3 sts).

Row 2: sl1, k2tog, psso and fasten off.

Making up

As for large owl.

Sheep

Materials:

Small amount of fleecy, chunky (bulky) yarn in white

Small amount of DK (8-ply) yarn in white

Small amounts of 4-ply (fingering) yarn in dark brown and red (or two strands taken from DK (8-ply) yarn)

Small amount of toy stuffing

Small bell

Additional equipment:

A pair of 4mm (US 6, UK 8) knitting needles

Approximate size:

6cm (2⅜in) long

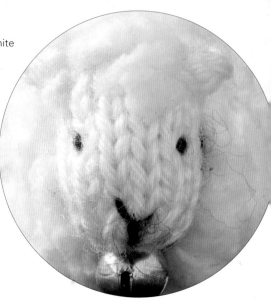

> ### Knitting note
> The body is knitted using fleecy, chunky (bulky) yarn with 4mm (US 6, UK 8) needles. The rest is knitted using white DK (8-ply) yarn with 2.75mm (US 2, UK 12) knitting needles.

Instructions:

Body

Cast on 15 sts using 4mm (US 6, UK 8) needles and fleecy white yarn and work in st st for 10 rows.

Break yarn, draw through sts, pull tightly and fasten off.

Head

Using white DK (8-ply) yarn, cast on 6 sts using 2.75mm (US 2, UK 12) knitting needles.

Row 1 (WS): p.

Row 2: inc to end (12 sts).

Rows 3–5: st st, starting with a p row.

Row 6: (k1, k2tog) to end (8 sts).

Break yarn, draw through sts, pull tightly and fasten off.

Ears (make two)

Cast on 2 sts using white DK (8-ply) yarn.

Row 1: p2tog and fasten off.

Making up

Using the cast-off end of the yarn, sew the body and stuff. Work a gathering thread along the cast-on edge and close the body seam. Using the cast-off end of the yarn, sew the head seam and stuff. Work a gathering thread along the cast-on edge and pull it tightly to close the head. Attach the head to the body. Attach the ears. Using 4-ply (fingering) dark brown yarn (or two strands taken from some dark brown DK (8-ply) yarn), work French knots for the eyes and backstitch for the nose, using the photograph above for guidance. Thread a small bell onto some red 4-ply (fingering) yarn and attach it to the neck.

Dice

Materials:

Approx. 40m (44yd) of DK (8-ply) yarn in green or coral

Approx. 10m (11yd) of DK (8-ply) yarn in green or coral

Small amount of toy stuffing

Approximate size:

4cm (1½in) across one side of dice

Instructions:

Body (make three)

Cast on 13 sts using yarn colour of your choice.

Rows 1–13: st st, starting with a p row.

Row 14 (WS): k to create a ridge for the edge.

Rows 15–28: st st, starting with a k row.

Cast off.

Dots (make 21)

Cast on 8 sts using green or coral yarn (opposite colour to body), break yarn. Draw yarn through sts, pull tightly and fasten off.

Making up

Gently steam the body pieces with a protecting cloth between the iron and the knitted piece. Sew the three pieces of the body together to make the six sides of the cube, and stuff. Attach the dots to the body, from one to six, ensuring that opposite sides add up to seven.

Chubby Bunny

Materials:

Approx. 12m (13yd) of DK (8-ply) yarn in beige

Small amounts of DK (8-ply) yarn in dark brown and coral

Small amount of toy stuffing

Approximate size:

9cm (3½in) high

Instructions:

Body

Cast on 7 sts using beige yarn.

Row 1 (WS): p.

Row 2: inc in each st (14 sts).

Row 3: p.

Row 4: (k1, inc) to end (21 sts).

Rows 5–9: st st, starting with a p row.

Row 10: (k2, k2tog) to last st, k1 (16 sts).

Row 11: p.

Row 12: (k2tog) to end (8 sts).

Break yarn, draw through sts, pull tightly and fasten off.

Head

Cast on 8 sts using beige yarn.

Row 1 (WS): p.

Row 2: inc in each st (16 sts).

Row 3: p.

Row 4: (k1, inc) to end (24 sts).

Rows 5–13: st st, starting with a p row.

Row 14: (k1, k2tog) to end (16 sts).

Row 15: (p2tog) to end (8 sts).

Break yarn, draw through sts, pull tightly and fasten off.

Legs (make two)

Cast on 8 sts using beige yarn and work in st st for 6 rows.

Row 7: (p2tog) to end (4 sts).

Break yarn, draw through sts, pull tightly and fasten off.

Arms (make two)

Cast on 7 sts using beige yarn and work in st st for 5 rows, starting with a p row.

Row 6: (p2tog) to last st, p1 (4 sts).

Break yarn, draw through sts, pull tightly and fasten off.

Ears (make two)

Cast on 10 sts using beige yarn.

Rows 1–5: st st, starting with a p row.

Row 6: (k2, k2tog) to end (8 sts).

Row 7: p.

Row 8: k2tog, (k1, k2tog) to end (5 sts).

Break yarn, draw through sts, pull tightly and fasten off.

Making up

Sew head, body and limbs, filling with toy stuffing as you go. Attach the parts to the body. Sew the ears, folding each piece in half, and attach them to the head without stuffing. Using dark brown yarn, make French knots for the eyes and backstitch straight lines for the nose and mouth, using the photographs for guidance. Using two strands taken from the coral yarn, backstitch three straight lines for each set of whiskers.

Guardsman

Materials:
Small amounts of DK (8-ply) yarn in black, dark brown, skin colour and red
Small amount of toy stuffing

Additional equipment:
3mm (US C/2 or D/3, UK 11) crochet hook
Spare needle or stitch holder

Approximate size:
9.5cm (3¾in) high

Instructions:

Right leg
Cast on 10 sts using dark brown yarn and work in st st for 6 rows. Break yarn, keep sts on a spare needle or a holder.

Left leg and body
Work as for the right leg, but do not break yarn.

Row 7: k5, yfwd, sl1, ybk, turn, sl1, p to end.

Place the right leg piece on the left side of the same needle and continue.

Row 8: with RS facing, k across both sections to connect the two legs (20 sts).

Row 9: p5, ybk, sl1, yfwd, turn, sl1, k to end.

Row 10: change to red yarn and p across.

Row 11: k14, yfwd, sl1, ybk, turn, sl1, p8, ybk, sl1, yfwd, turn, sl1, k to end.

Rows 12–15: st st, starting with a p row.

Row 16: (p2tog) to end (10 sts).

Row 17: change to skin colour yarn and k.

Row 18: inc in each st (20 sts).

Rows 19–26: st st.

Row 27: (k2tog) to end (10 sts).

Break yarn, draw through sts, pull tight and fasten off.

Arms (make two)
Cast on 6 sts using red yarn and work st st for 5 rows. Change to skin colour yarn and work two more rows. Break yarn, draw through sts, pull tight and fasten off.

Hat
Cast on 22 sts using black yarn and work in st st for 14 rows.

Row 15: k2, (k2tog, k2) to end (17 sts).

Break yarn, draw through sts, pull tight and fasten off.

Strap
Make 20 chains with the crochet hook, using black yarn.

Making up
Using the cast-off end of yarn, sew the head seam. Sew each leg, using the cast-on end of the yarn. Stuff the leg and head. Stuff the body, avoiding the neck area, and close the seam. Using the skin colour yarn, work a gathering thread around the neck and pull tightly to shape. Sew the hat seam, stuff the top part of the hat lightly and attach it to the head with the seam at the back. Attach the strap. Sew the arm seams and the attach the arms to the body. Make two French knots for buttons and two for the eyes using dark brown yarn. For the nose, backstitch the same spot two or three times using skin colour yarn.

Pretty Piggy

Materials:

Approx. 10m (11yd) of DK (8-ply) yarn in pink

Small amounts of DK (8-ply) yarn in dark brown and soft pink

Small amounts of 4-ply (fingering) yarn in cerise, yellow, green and purple or colours of your choice for the flowers (use two or three strands of DK (8-ply) yarn if you do not have 4-ply (fingering) yarn)

Small amount of toy stuffing

Approximate size:

6.5cm (2½in) long

Instructions:

Body

Cast on 8 sts loosely using pink yarn.

Row 1 (RS): inc to end (16 sts).

Row 2: p.

Row 3: inc to end (32 sts).

Rows 4–20: st st, starting with a p row.

Row 21: k10, (k2tog, k1) four times, k10 (28 sts).

Row 22: p.

Row 23: (k2tog) to end (14 sts).

Row 24: change to soft pink yarn and p.

Row 25: p for the edge.

Row 26: p2, (p2tog, p2) to end (11 sts).

Break yarn, draw through sts, pull tightly and fasten off.

Ears (make two)

Cast on 5 sts using pink yarn.

Row 1 (WS): p.

Row 2: skpo, k1, k2tog (3 sts).

Row 3: p.

Row 4: sl1, k2tog, psso and fasten off.

Legs (make four)

Cast on 5 sts using pink yarn and work an i-cord for 2 rows. Break yarn, draw through sts, pull tightly and fasten off.

Flowers (make two)

Cast on 10 sts using 4-ply (fingering) yarn colour of your choice, break yarn. Draw through sts, pull tightly and fasten off.

Making up

Sew the body seam and stuff. Attach the legs and tail. Fold the ears in half and attach. Thread some 4-ply (fingering) yarn in the colour of your choice onto a sewing needle and insert into the centre of the flower, making a short backstitch. Attach the flowers above the piggy's right ear. Work French knots for the eyes using dark brown yarn. Work small backstitches for the nostrils and mouth using dark brown yarn.

Wristwatch

Materials:

Small amounts of DK (8-ply) yarn in yellow, pink, green, red, blue and brown (or colours of your choice)

2.5cm (1in) diameter circle of lightweight cardboard

2 x 1cm (⅜in) strips of Velcro

Blue (or yellow) sewing thread

Approximate size:

Strap 14cm (5½in) long; watchface 3.5cm (1⅜in) in diameter

Instructions:

To make blue wristwatch:

Watch face

Cast on 11 sts using yellow yarn.

Row 1 (WS): p.

Row 2: inc in each st (22 sts).

Rows 3–8: st st, starting with a p row.

Row 9: (p2tog) to end (11 sts).

Break yarn, draw through sts, pull tightly and fasten off.

Face edging

Cast on 22 sts using pink yarn and work st st for 3 rows, starting with a p row. Cast off.

Enclose the cardboard inside the face and sew the seam. Attach the edging around the face.

Winder

Cast on 5 sts using green yarn. Break yarn, draw through sts and pull tightly. Attach it to the watch face edging.

Strap

Cast on 6 sts using blue yarn and work in g st until the piece measures 14cm (5½in) or desired length. Cast off.

Making up

Embroider the face using brown yarn for the watch hands, and red French knots on the quarter hour marks. Attach the watch face to the strap. Attach a piece of Velcro at either end, one on top and the other underneath the strap, to close it.

To make the wristwatch in the alternative colourway, substitute yellow yarn for the strap, and follow the colours for the watch face using the photographs for guidance.

Cheeky Monkey

Materials:

Approx. 8m (9yd) of DK (8-ply) yarn in brown

Small amounts of DK (8-ply) yarn in dark brown and skin colour

Small amount of toy stuffing

Approximate size:

4.5cm (1¾in) high

Instructions:

Body

Cast on 7 sts using brown yarn.

Row 1 (WS): p.

Row 2: inc in each st (14 sts).

Row 3: p.

Row 4: (k1, inc) to end (21 sts).

Rows 5–15: st st, starting with a p row.

Row 16: (k1, k2tog, k1) to last st, k1 (16 sts).

Row 17: p.

Row 18: k1, (k2tog, k1) to end (11 sts).

Break yarn, draw through sts, pull tightly and fasten off.

Face

The face is made up of two small circles around the eyes and one larger half-circle to go around the mouth.

Circles around the eyes (make two)

Using two strands taken from the skin colour yarn, cast on 8 sts, break yarn, draw through sts, pull tightly and fasten off. Insert the threaded needle back into the stitches and pull to close the end. Secure the edges with a stitch to make the piece into a small circle.

Half-circle for the mouth

Using two strands taken from the skin colour yarn, cast on 10 sts and p 1 row. Break yarn, draw through sts, insert the needle back into the sts and pull to close the end.

Ears (make two)

Using two strands taken from the skin colour yarn, cast on 10 sts, break yarn and draw through sts. Insert the needle back into the sts and pull to close the end.

Tail

Cast on 2 sts using brown yarn and work an i-cord for 9 rows. Fasten off.

Making up

Sew the body seam and stuff. To flatten the base, insert a threaded needle from the centre of the base and take it out from the back of the body and repeat. Pull gently. Attach the two small circles for the eyes and the half-circle to the mouth area. Using two strands taken from the dark brown yarn, work French knots for the eyes and make short backstitches for the nostrils. Backstitch a curve for the mouth with the same yarn. Attach the ears and the tail.

To make the monkey in the alternative colourway, simply use a reddish-brown DK (8-ply) yarn instead of brown.

Flying Saucer

Materials:

Approx. 20m (22yd) of DK (8-ply) yarn in grey

Small amounts of DK (8-ply) yarn in red, orange, light blue, light green and yellow

8cm (3⅛in) diameter circle of lightweight cardboard

Small amount of toy stuffing

Approximate size:

8cm (3⅛in) diameter, 7cm (2¾in) high

Instructions:

Top compartment

Loosely cast on 7 sts using grey yarn.

Row 1 (RS): inc in each st (14 sts).

Row 2: p.

Row 3: (k1, inc) to end (21 sts).

Row 4: p.

Row 5: (k2, inc) to end (28 sts).

Row 6: p.

Row 7: (k3, inc) to end (35 sts).

Row 8: k for the edge.

Rows 9–16: st st, starting with a k row.

Row 17: (k3, k2tog) to end (28 sts).

Row 18: p.

Row 19: (k2, k2tog) to end (21 sts).

Row 20: p.

Row 21: (k1, k2tog) to end (14 sts).

Row 22: p.

Row 23: (k2tog) to end (7 sts).

Row 24: p.

Break yarn, draw through sts, pull tightly and fasten off. Sew the seam, using the cast-off end. Stuff, and work a gathering thread along the cast-on edge to close.

Disc

Follow the pattern for the top compartment to Row 7 using grey yarn.

Row 8: p.

Row 9: (k4, inc) to end (42 sts).

Row 10: p.

Row 11: (k5, inc) to end (49 sts).

Row 12: p.

Row 13: change to red yarn and (k6, inc) to end (56 sts).

Row 14: k for the edge.

Rows 15 and 16: st st.

Row 17: (k6, k2tog) to end (49 sts).

Row 18: p.

Row 19: (k5, k2tog) to end (42 sts).

Row 20: p.

Row 21: change to orange yarn and (k4, k2tog) to end (35 sts).

Row 22: p.

Row 23: (k3, k2tog) to end (28 sts).

Row 24: p.

Row 25: (k2, k2tog) to end (21 sts).

Row 26: p.

Row 27: (k1, k2tog) to end (14 sts).

Row 28: p.

Row 29: (k2tog) to end (7 sts).

Break yarn, draw through sts, pull tightly and fasten off. Sew the seam using both cast-off and cast-on ends. Insert the cardboard and close the seam.

Windows (make 5)

Cast on 10 sts using light blue yarn and k 1 row. Break yarn, draw through sts, pull tightly and fasten off. Insert the threaded needle back into sts to close the circle.

Bottom piece (make 3)

Loosely cast on 6 sts using yellow yarn.

Row 1 (RS): inc in each st (12 sts).

Row 2: p.

Row 3: (k1, inc) to end (18 sts).

Row 4: k for the edge.

Rows 5–9: st st, starting with a k row.

Row 10: p2, (p2tog, p2) to end (14 sts).

Break yarn, draw through sts, pull tightly and fasten off. Sew the seam, using the cast-off end of yarn. Stuff and work a gathering thread along the cast-on edge to close.

Antenna

Cast on 2 sts using light green yarn and work an i-cord for 8 rows. Fasten off.

Cast on 6 sts using yellow yarn. Break yarn, draw through sts, and pull tightly. Attach it to the end of the cord.

Making up

Attach the antenna, then the windows, spacing them evenly round the top section. Attach the disc and bottom pieces.

Penguin

Materials:

Small amounts of DK (8-ply) yarn in grey, yellow, white and dark brown

Small amount of toy stuffing

Approximate size:

5cm (2in) high

Instructions:

Body

Starting at the base, cast on 7 sts using grey yarn.

Row 1 (WS): p.

Row 2: inc in each st (14 sts).

Row 3: p.

Row 4: (k1, inc) to end (21 sts).

Row 5: p7 (grey), p7 (white), p7 (grey).

Rows 6–11: keeping the colours as set, st st.

Row 12: k2, k2tog, k3 (grey), k1, (k2tog, k1) twice (white), k3, k2tog, k2 (grey) (17 sts).

Row 13: p2 (grey), p13 (white), p2 (grey).

Rows 14–16: keeping the colours as set, st st.

Row 17: p3 (grey), p4 (white), p3 (grey), p4 (white), p3 (grey).

Rows 18 and 19: keeping the colours as set, st st.

Rows 20–22: st st with grey yarn only.

Row 23: (p2, p2tog) to last st, p1 (13 sts).

Break yarn, draw through sts, pull tightly and fasten off.

Wings (make two)

Cast on 8 sts using grey yarn.

Rows 1 and 2: st st, starting with a p row.

Row 3: p1, p2tog, p2, p2tog, p1 (6 sts).

Row 4: k.

Break yarn, draw through sts, pull tightly and fasten off.

Beak

Cast on 5 sts using yellow yarn.

Row 1: p2tog, p1, p2tog (3 sts).

Row 2: skpo, k1, pass the first st over the second and fasten off.

Feet (make two)

Cast on 4 sts using yellow yarn.

Rows 1 and 2: k.

Row 3: k1, k2tog, k1 (3 sts).

Row 4: k.

Cast off.

Making up

Sew the body seam and stuff. Sew the wing seams and attach a wing to either side of the body without stuffing. Attach the beak. Attach the feet with the cast-on edge facing forwards. Work French knots for the eyes using dark brown yarn.

To make the blue penguin follow the pattern, substituting blue yarn for grey.

Country Boy and Girl

Materials:

Small amounts of DK (8-ply) yarn in skin colour, light blue, soft pink, caramel, light brown and dark brown

Small amount of toy stuffing

Instructions:

Boy's body and head

Starting with the left leg, cast on 12 sts using light blue yarn.

Rows 1–4: st st, starting with a p row.

Row 5: p2, (p2tog four times, p2 (8 sts).

Row 6: k2, (inc, k2) to end (10sts).

Rows 7–10: st st, starting with a p row.

Break yarn, keep sts on a spare needle or a stitch holder.

Right leg

Work as for the left leg, but do not break yarn.

Row 11 (WS): p across the right leg then the left leg to connect the pieces (20 sts).

Row 12: k.

Row 13: k.

Rows 14–19: with RS facing, join caramel yarn and work in st st, starting with a k row.

Row 20 (shape neck): (k1, k2tog) three times, (k2tog) twice, (k1, k2tog) twice, k1 (13 sts).

Row 21: change to skin colour yarn and p.

Row 22: k3, (inc) seven times, k3 (20sts).

Rows 23–26: st st, starting with a p row.

Row 27(shape eyeline): p3, (p2tog, p1) to last 5 sts, p2tog, p3 (15 sts).

Rows 28–31: st st.

Row 32: k2, (k2tog, k2) to last st, k1 (12 sts).

Break yarn, draw through sts, pull tightly and fasten off.

Arms (make two)

Cast on 7 sts using caramel yarn and work in st st for 5 rows. Change to skin colour yarn and work in st st for 2 rows, starting with a p row. Break yarn, draw through sts, pull tightly and fasten off.

Additional equipment:

3mm (US C/2 or D/3, UK 11) crochet hook
Spare needle or stitch holder

Approximate size:

7.5cm (3in) high

Hat

Cast on 10 sts using light blue yarn.

Row 1 (WS): p.

Row 2: (inc) to end (20 sts).

Row 3: p.

Row 4: k.

Row 5: cast off 6 sts, k7, cast off to end purlwise (8 sts).

Row 6: with RS facing, join yarn and k.

Row 7: p2tog, p to last 2 sts, p2tog (6 sts).

Cast off.

Straps (make two)

With the crochet hook and light blue yarn, work 14 chains, fasten off.

Making up

Using the cast-off end of yarn, sew the head seam. Using the cast-on end of yarn, sew each leg. Stuff the head, legs and body and close the seam. Avoid stuffing the neck area. Using the skin colour yarn, work a gathering thread around the neck and pull tightly to shape. Work a gathering thread around the decrease row of the face to create the eye line indent. Work a few backstitches on the front of the foot to shape the ankles. Sew the arm seam and attach the arms to the body. Using light brown yarn, work backstitches on the sides of the head, leaving loops for the hair. Attach the hat. Using dark brown yarn, make two French knots for the eyes. To create the nose, backstitch the same spot two or three times using skin colour yarn.

Girl

Work all sections as given for the boy, using soft pink yarn instead of blue. For the hair, make loops at the front for her fringe, then make long loops at the sides and work them into braids. Secure the braid ends with soft pink yarn.

Fox

Materials:

Approx. 30m (33yd) of DK (8-ply) yarn in light brown

Small amounts of DK (8-ply) yarn in white, dark brown and brown

Small amount of 4-ply (fingering) yarn in brown

Small amount of toy stuffing

Approximate size:

8cm (3⅛in) high

Instructions:

Body

Starting with the base, cast on 7 sts using light brown yarn.

Row 1 (WS): p.

Row 2: inc in each st (14 sts).

Row 3: p.

Row 4: (k1, inc) to end (21 sts).

Rows 5–7: st st, starting with a p row.

Row 8: k9 (light brown), k3 (white), k9 (light brown).

Row 9: p8 (light brown), p5 (white), p8 (light brown).

Row 10: k7 (light brown), k7 (white), k7 (light brown).

Rows 11–16: keeping the colours as set, work in st st starting with a p row.

Row 17: with light brown yarn only (p1, p2tog) to end (14 sts).

Break yarn, draw through sts, pull tightly and fasten off.

Head

Cast on 8 sts using light brown yarn.

Row 1 (WS): p.

Row 2: inc in each st (16 sts).

Row 3: p.

Row 4: (k1, inc) to end (24 sts).

Rows 5–7: st st, starting with a p row.

Row 8: (k2, k2tog) to end (18 sts).

Rows 9–13: st st, starting with a p row.

Row 14: (k1, k2tog) to end (12 sts).

Break yarn, draw through sts, pull tightly and fasten off.

Muzzle

Cast on 10 sts using white yarn and p 1 row. Break yarn, draw through sts, pull tightly and fasten off.

Ears (make two)

Cast on 7 sts using light brown yarn and p 1 row.

Row 2: change to white yarn and k1, (k2tog, k1) to end (5 sts).

Break yarn, draw through sts, pull tightly and fasten off.

Arms (make two)

Cast on 5 sts using light brown yarn and work an i-cord for 4 rows. Change to dark brown yarn and work 1 more row. Break yarn, draw through sts, pull tightly and fasten off.

Legs (make two)

Cast on 8 sts using light brown yarn.

Row 1 (WS): p.

Row 2: k.

Row 3: (p1, inc) 3 times, p2 (11 sts).

Rows 4–6: st st.

Row 7: change to dark brown yarn and p.

Row 8: k2, k2tog, k3, k2tog, k2 (9 sts).

Break yarn, thread sts through a sewing needle, draw up tightly.

Tail

Cast on 10 sts using light brown yarn.

Rows 1–4: st st, starting with a p row.

Row 5: (p1, inc) to end (15 sts).

Rows 6–9: st st.

Row 10: change to white yarn and k.

Row 11: (p2, inc) to end (20 sts).

Row 12: k.

Row 13: (p1, 2tog) to last 2 sts, p2 (14 sts).

Row 14: (k2tog) to end (7 sts).

Break yarn, draw through sts, pull tightly and fasten off.

Scarf

Cast on 3 sts using 4-ply (fingering) brown yarn and work in g st until the work measures 11cm (4¼in). Cast off. To make the fringe, thread a length of the same yarn and backstitch across each end, leaving a loop every other stitch. Repeat four or five times across each edge. Cut the loops.

Making up

Sew the body, head, leg and tail seams and stuff. Attach the body parts to the body. Attach the muzzle and ears. Using dark brown yarn, work French knots for the eyes and backstitch the nose and mouth. Tie the scarf around the fox's neck.

Skittles and Ball

Materials:

Approx. 40m (44yd) DK (8-ply) yarn in caramel (makes a set of 7)

Small amounts of DK (8-ply) yarn in red, blue, yellow, orange, green, light blue and purple

Small amount of toy stuffing

Approximate size:

Skittle: 6cm (2⅜in); ball: 3cm (1¼in) diameter

Instructions:

Skittles

Cast on 8 sts using caramel yarn.

Row 1 (WS): p.

Row 2: inc in each st. (16 sts)

Rows 3 and 4: st st, starting with a p row.

Row 5: k to make a ridge for the edge of the skittle.

Rows 6 and 7: st st., starting with a k row.

Row 8: (k2, inc) to last st, k1 (21 sts).

Rows 9–17: st st, starting with a p row.

Row 18: using contrast colour yarn, k.

Row 19: (p2tog) to last st, p1 (11 sts). Do not break yarn.

Rows 20 and 21: using caramel yarn, st st. Do not break yarn.

Row 22: using contrast colour yarn left at row 19, k. Break yarn, leaving a long end.

Row 23: move sts to other end of DPN. Using caramel yarn left at row 21, k.

Row 24: p1 (inc, p1) to end (16 sts).

Rows 25–30: st st.

Row 31: (k2tog) to end (8 sts).

Break yarn, draw through sts, pull tightly and fasten off.

Making up

Sew the body seam and stuff. Insert a threaded needle into the body from the base centre and take it out through the back of the skittle and repeat. Pull gently to flatten the base. Fasten off. Using the contrast colour yarn left at row 19, thread through every stitch on the same row to enhance the colour. Fasten off.

Ball

Using red or blue yarn, cast on 10 sts.

Row 1 (WS): p.

Row 2: inc to end (20 sts).

Rows 3–10: st st, starting with a p row.

Row 11: (p2tog) to end (10 sts).

Fasten off.

Making up

With the fastened-off yarn end, sew the body and stuff. Work a gathering thread around the cast-on edge and draw tightly to close the ball.

Goldfish

Materials:

Approx. 10m (11yd) of DK (8-ply) yarn in body colour of your choice

Small amounts of 4-ply (fingering) yarn in white and black

Small amount of toy stuffing

Approximate size:

5cm (2in) long

Instructions:

Body

Cast on 5 sts using body colour yarn (use the same colour for tail and fins).

Row 1 (WS): p.

Row 2: inc to end (10 sts).

Row 3: p.

Row 4: (k1, inc) to end (15 sts).

Row 5: p.

Row 6: (k2, inc) to end (20 sts).

Rows 7–13: st st.

Row 14: (k1, k2tog, k1) to end (15 sts).

Row 15: (p1, p2tog) to end (10 sts).

Break yarn, draw through sts, pull tightly and fasten off.

Tail

First, work the two side sections (make two):

Cast on 3 sts and work in st st for 4 rows, starting with a p row.

Row 5: p2tog, p1 (2 sts).

Break yarn, draw through sts, pull tightly and fasten off.

To make the centre part of the tail:

Cast on 4 sts and work in st st for 5 rows, starting with a p row.

Row 6: skpo, k2tog (2 sts).

Row 7: p2tog and fasten off.

Fins (make two)

Cast on 3 sts and work in st st for 2 rows, starting with a p row.

Row 3: p3tog and fasten off.

Eyes (make two)

Using white 4-ply (fingering) yarn, cast on 8 sts. Break yarn, draw through sts, pull tightly and fasten off.

Making up

Sew the body seam and stuff. Attach the three tail sections and the fins. Attach the eyes. Using black 4-ply (fingering) yarn, work a French knot in the centre of the eyes.

Boy Angel

Materials:

Approx. 10m (11yd) of DK (8-ply) yarn
  in skin colour

Small amount of DK (8-ply) yarn in
  dark brown

Small amount of fleecy, chunky (bulky) yarn
  in white

Small amount of 4-ply (fingering) yarn
  in caramel

Small amount of toy stuffing

Approximate size:

5cm (2in) high

Instructions:

Body and head

Cast on 6 sts using skin colour yarn.

Row 1 (WS): p.

Row 2: inc to end (12 sts).

Row 3: p.

Row 4: (k1, inc) to end (18 sts).

Rows 5–11: st st, starting with a p row.

Row 12 (shape neck): (k1, k2tog) to end (12 sts).

Row 13: p.

Row 14: k3, (inc) six times, k3 (18 sts).

Rows 15–17: st st, starting with a p row.

Row 18 (shape eyeline): k3, (k2tog, k1) four
times, k3 (14 sts).

Rows 19–21: st st, starting with a p row.

Row 22: (k2, k2tog) to last 2 sts, k2 (11 sts).

Legs (make two)

Cast on 7 sts using skin colour yarn.

Rows 1–3: st st, starting with a p row.

Row 4: k2, k3tog, k2 (5 sts).

Row 5: p.

Row 6: inc, k to last st, inc (7 sts).

Rows 7 and 8: st st, starting with a p row.

Break yarn, draw through sts, pull tightly and
fasten off.

Arms (make two)

Cast on 4 sts using skin colour yarn and work an
i-cord for 4 rows. Break yarn, draw through sts,
pull tightly and fasten off.

Wings (make two)

Cast on 12 sts using fleecy white yarn.

Row 1: k.

Row 2: skpo, k to last 2 sts, k2tog (10 sts).

Rows 3–5: repeat row 2 (4 sts).

Row 6: k.

Cast off.

Making up

Sew the head seam from the cast-off end.
Using the cast-on end of yarn, work a gathering
thread along the cast-on edge and pull tightly.
Sew the rest of the body seam and stuff,
avoiding the neck area. Work a gathering
thread along the neck and pull tightly to shape.
From the centre of the angel's bottom, insert
a threaded needle and take it out through the
back of the neck and repeat. Pull gently to
flatten the base. Using skin colour yarn, work
a gathering thread over row 18 and pull to
create the eyeline. Sew arm and leg seams and
attach them to the body. Using caramel 4-ply
(fingering) yarn, work backstitch on the head,
leaving a loop every other stitch. Attach the
wings. Using dark brown yarn, make French
knots for eyes. For the nose, backstitch three
times in the same spot with skin colour yarn.

Little Beagle

Materials:

Small amounts of DK (8-ply) yarn in black, brown and white (or colours of your choice – approx. 20m (22yd) makes one dog)

Small amount of toy stuffing

Approximate size:

6cm (2⅜ in) high

Instructions:

Body (black, white and brown dog)

Cast on 7 sts using black yarn.

Row 1 (WS): p.

Row 2: (inc) in each st (14 sts).

Row 3: p.

Row 4: (k1, inc) to end (21 sts).

Row 5: p7 (black), p7 (white), p7 (black).

Rows 6–9: keeping the colours as set, work in st st.

Row 10: (k2, k2tog) twice in black, k2, k2tog, k1 in white, (k2tog, k2) twice in black (16 sts).

Row 11: keeping the colours as set, p.

Row 12: (k2tog) to end with black (8 sts).

Break yarn, draw through sts, pull tightly and fasten off.

Head

Cast on 8 sts using black yarn.

Row 1 (WS): p.

Row 2: (inc) in each st (16 sts).

Row 3: p.

Row 4: (k1, inc) to end (24 sts).

Row 5: p3 (black), p8 (brown), p2 (black), p8 (brown), p3 (black).

Rows 6–13: keeping the colours as set, work in st st.

Row 14: break brown yarn, (k1, k2tog) to end with black only (16 sts).

Row 15: (p2tog) to end (8 sts).

Break yarn, draw through sts, pull tightly and fasten off.

Back legs (make two)

Cast on 8 sts using black yarn and work in st st for 2 rows, starting with p row. Change to white yarn and work 2 more rows in st st.

Row 5: (p2tog) to end (4 sts).

Break yarn, draw through sts, pull tightly and fasten off.

Front legs (make two)

Cast on 7 sts using black yarn and work in st st for 2 rows. Change to white yarn and work 2 more rows in st st.

Break yarn, draw through sts, pull tightly and fasten off.

Ears (make two)

Cast on 10 sts using black yarn.

Row 1–4: st st, starting with a p row.

Row 5: p2, (p2tog, p2) to end (8 sts).

Row 7: k.

Break yarn, draw through sts, pull tightly and fasten off.

Tail

Work as for front leg but do not stuff.

Muzzle

Cast on 18 sts using white yarn.

Row 1 (WS): p.

Row 2: (k2, k2tog) to last 2 sts, k2 (14 sts).

Row 3: (p2tog) to end (7 sts).

Break yarn, draw through sts, pull tightly and fasten off.

Variations

A: Beige dog with rust ears

Knit the head, body and legs using beige yarn only. Knit the tail and ears in rust yarn, and the muzzle in white.

Work small ears as follows:

Cast on 8 sts using rust yarn.

Row 1 (WS): p.

Row 2: k.

Row 3: p2, (p2tog) twice, p2. (6 sts)

Break yarn, draw through sts, pull tightly and fasten off.

B: Brown and light brown dog

Work the body in brown and beige yarn. Using brown yarn, follow the head pattern given except:

Row 5: p11 (brown), p2 (beige), p11 (brown).

Work the legs and muzzle in beige yarn. Work the ears and tail in dark brown yarn.

Making up

Sew head, body and leg pieces and stuff. Attach all body parts to the body. Do not stuff the ears, tail and muzzle. Work French knots in brown yarn for the eyes and backstitch the nose and mouth.

Clown

Materials:

Small amounts of DK (8-ply) yarn in yellow, orange, pink, light green, light purple, dark brown and skin colour (or colours of your choice)

Small amount of 4-ply (fingering) yarn in yellow (or two strands taken from DK (8-ply) yarn)

Small amount of toy stuffing

Approximate size:

9cm (3½in) high

Instructions:

Body and head

Cast on 7 sts using pink yarn.

Row 1 (WS): p.

Row 2: inc in each st (14 sts).

Row 3: p.

Row 4: (k1, inc) to end (21 sts).

Rows 5–9: st st, starting with a p row.

Row 10: (k4, k2tog) three times, k3 (18 sts).

Rows 11–13: st st, starting with a p row.

Row 14 (shape neck): (k1, k2tog) to end (12 sts).

Row 15: change to the skin colour yarn and p.

Row 16 (shape eyeline): k3, (inc) six times, k3 (18 sts).

Rows 17–19: st st, starting with a p row.

Row 20: k3, (k2tog, k1) four times, k3 (14 sts).

Rows 21–23: st st, starting with a p row.

Row 24: (k2, k2tog) to last 2 sts, k2 (11 sts).

Break yarn, draw through sts, pull tightly and fasten off.

Legs (make two)

Cast on 8 sts using light purple yarn.

Row 1 (WS): p.

Row 2: inc in each st (16 sts).

Rows 3–5: st st, starting with a p row.

Row 6: (k2, k2tog) to end (12 sts).

Row 7: p.

Break yarn, draw through sts, pull tightly and fasten off.

Feet (make two)

Cast on 4 sts using yellow yarn, and work an i-cord for 3 rows.

Row 4: k1, k2tog, k1 (3 sts).

Row 5: sl1, k2tog, psso and fasten off.

Arms (make two)

Cast on 7 sts using light green yarn.

Row 1 (RS): inc in each st (14 sts).

Rows 2–4: st st, starting with a p row.

Row 5: (k2tog) to end (7 sts).

Hands (make two)

Cast on 3 sts using skin colour yarn, and work an i-cord for 4 rows. Break yarn, draw through sts, pull tightly and fasten off.

Hat

Cast on 18 sts using orange yarn.

Rows 1–6: st st.

Row 7: k2, (k2tog, k2) to end (14 sts).

Rows 8–11: st st, starting with a p row.

Row 12: (p2tog) to end (7 sts).

Break yarn, draw through sts, pull tightly and fasten off.

Making up

Sew the head, using the cast-off end of yarn. Using the cast-on end of yarn, work a gathering thread along the cast-on edge and pull tightly. Sew the rest of the body, leaving an opening for the stuffing. Stuff the body and head, avoiding the neck area. Close the seam. Work a gathering thread around the neck and pull to shape. Work a gathering thread to create an eye line if desired. Sew the leg seams, stuff and attach a foot on one end. Attach the legs to the body. Place the hand inside the arm, sew the arm seam and stuff. Attach to the body. Sew the hat and attach it to the head with the seam at the back. Using dark brown yarn, work French knots for the eyes. To create the nose, backstitch the same spot two or three times using skin colour yarn. Using 4-ply (fingering) yellow yarn or two strands taken from yellow DK (8-ply) yarn, backstitch the hair at the front of the head, leaving loops every other stitch.

Acknowledgements

I would like to thank everyone in the Search Press team, especially Katie French and May Corfield, for helping me to create such a wonderful book. I would also like to thank the designer, Juan Hayward, for the beautiful layout and Paul Bricknell for the photography.

Publishers' Note

If you would like more information on knitting techniques try: *Knitting for the Absolute Beginner* by Alison Dupernex, Search Press, 2012; or *Twenty to Make: Easy Knitted Scarves* by Monica Russel, Search Press, 2013